D1006598

A SPECIAL GIFT

FOR

David + Bev Donnelly

FROM

Maggie Herrick

DATE

Christmas 1998

Copyright © 1998

Brownlow Publishing Company
6309 Airport Freeway
Fort Worth, TX 76117

ISBN: 1-57051-143-8

Printed in Singapore

Cover/Interior:
Koechel Peterson & Associates

THEY CALL IT GOLF

Brownlow

T his collection of inspirational books, journals and note pads from Brownlow features vintage images that celebrate golf's Scottish heritage.

A hundred years ago, as golf was rapidly expanding into North America and other parts of the world, no one would have predicted the game's present popularity. To its devoted fans and players we dedicate this series.

IN EARLIEST TIMES, CERTAIN
NATIVE TRIBES PRACTICED
THE STRANGE CUSTOM OF
BEATING THE GROUND WITH
CLUBS AND UTTERING WILD,
BLOODCURDLING YELLS.
ANTHROPOLOGISTS
CALLED IT A FORM OF
PRIMITIVE EXPRESSION.
TODAY THEY CALL IT GOLF.

THE GAME OF GOLF

Gifted writers have probed into the origin of the Game of Golf and have attributed its derivation to the French games of *la chole*, *jeu de mail*, and to the Dutch game of *het kolven*. On the other hand, some state that it originated amongst Scottish shepherd boys knocking stones into holes with their crooks to wile away time whilst watching their flocks. As yet, no one seems to have established beyond all reasonable doubt its true origin. Records show beyond dispute, however, that golf has been played in Scotland since 1457, and it is believed to have been played there as early as 1100.

J. a. Storer Carson

Former Secretary of the Royal and Ancient Golf Club of St. Andrews

The Royal and Ancient Golf Club of St. Andrews

• Old Tom Morris, *Open Champion 1861, 1862, 1864, 18*

NOT BY GOLF ALONE

Golf might well have died out entirely in Scotland between 1750 and 1850 as the royals and aristocrats showed little interest in golf, while the lower classes could not afford it.

However, a few clubs in Scotland continued to play golf mainly as a way of stimulating their appetites and providing a suitable opportunity for a wager. The minutes for one meeting of the North Berwick Golf Club in 1832 contain only 10 words about golf, but many long details are discussed about the menu and food preparations for the next meeting. At that meeting, mutton, pickled pork, whiskey, champagne, and a haggis were to be devoured. After all, man cannot live by golf alone.

THE GOLF COURSE

While setting forth some of the advantages to be derived from the game of golf, it occurred to me, "Are there no disadvantages?" I have come to the conclusion there are none, and I am able to suggest only one difficulty: that of obtaining the required amount of space to play the game according to its true and primitive character. A cricket-field, a tennis-ground, or space for football matches can easily be found anywhere. But a golf course is not so easily to be met with, for a vast expanse of grassy turf is absolutely indispensable. The ground should be of an undulating character and abound in hazards of every description. Golf links of that character are found chiefly by the seaside, especially on the east coast of Scotland. Similar places are on the coasts of England, where many of them are now being appropriated to golf because of the growing popularity of this most fascinating game.

W. T. Linskill, *Founder of the Cambridge University Golf Club*

THE DANGERS OF GOLF

Excessive golfing dwarfs the intellect. Nor is this to be wondered at when we consider that the more fatuously vacant the mind is, the better for play. It has been observed that absolute idiots play the steadiest.

Sir Walter Simpson

Golf appeals to the idiot in us and the child. What child does not grasp the pleasure principle of miniature golf? Just how childlike golf players become is proven by their frequent inability to count past five.

John Updike

...ng Tom Morris, *Open Champion 1868, 1869, 1870, 1872* •

I have always thought that Young Tom Morris was the greatest golfer that ever lived. Now I believe that Bobby Jones is equally wonderful. He is the reincarnation of Young Tom. I have known both more or less intimately and I am familiar with the conditions under which each played: Young Tom on an unkempt, rough course with the gutta ball, Bobby on a smooth, parklike perfectly kept course with the rubber-cored ball. To my mind, these two are the greatest golfers in history, both as to execution, clean sportsmanship, courtesy, equable temperament, and personality.

Charles Blair MacDonald

SELF-CONTROL

Every golfer can expect to have
four bad shots a round. When you do,
just put them out of your mind.

Walter Hagen

Buy the truth and do not sell it; get wisdom,
discipline and understanding.

Proverbs 23:23

For a man to conquer himself is the first
and noblest of all victories.

Plato

• Willie Park, Sr., *first Open Champion, 1860* •

AVOID
THE PRESS

Above all things do I implore players not to "press." Not only is it unnecessary, but is calculated to disturb the smoothness of the swing. Once you "press" you lose control of the shot. Let the club head follow through to the natural completion of the arc.

It is a mistake to think that brute force will add distance to your tee shot. Sacrifice sheer strength and concentrate upon perfect timing of contact with club and ball.

A.G. Haver, *1923 British Open Champion, Royal Troon*

Royal Troon *hosted its first Open in 1923.*

SECRETS OF THE GAME

Keep on hitting it straight until
the wee ball goes in the hole.

James Braid

Golfers have analyzed the game in order
to find "the secret." There is no secret.

Henry Cotton

The secret of good golf is to hit the ball hard,
straight, and not too often.

Anonymous

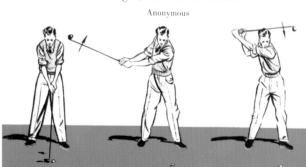

EARLY DEVELOPMENTS

Two of the oldest, but not as well known, Scottish golf clubs both made interesting contributions to the early game. In 1783, the Royal Aberdeen Golf Club (begun in 1780) introduced the five-minute limit on searching for lost golf balls.

And in 1874, the Crail Golfing Society (founded in 1786) began the practice of inserting metal cups inside the holes on the greens. In the meeting of August 7, 1874, the Society stipulated that "iron cases be got for the eight holes on the links to prevent the holes from being destroyed."

Golfers are the greatest worriers in the world of sport.

Billy Casper

Worry is an indication that we think God cannot look after us.

Oswald Chambers

An anxious heart weighs a man down, but a kind word cheers him up.

Proverbs 12:25

Handling pressure is the difference between winning and losing.

Raymond Floyd

F. G. Tait, *the most popular golfer of his day*

H.R.H. The Prince of Wales, *Captain of the Royal and Ancient Golf Club, in 1922*

Golf is a game kings and presidents play
when they get tired of running countries.

Charles Price

A good golf course is like good music.
It does not necessarily appeal
the first time one plays it.

Alister MacKenzie

Golf is an easy game; it's just hard to play.

Anonymous.

Golf, like measles, should be caught young.

P. G. Wodehouse

UNWRITTEN RULES OF GOLF

The uglier a man's legs are,
the better he plays golf.

It's often necessary to hit a second drive
to really appreciate the first one.

The more often your opponent quotes the rules,
the greater the certainty that he cheats.

It takes 17 holes to get really warmed up.

Real golfers don't cry when
they line up their fourth putt.

Beyond the fact that it is a limitless arena
for the full play of human nature, there is
no sure accounting for golf's fascination.
Perhaps it is nothing more than the
best game man has ever devised.

Herbert Warren Wind

In golf, there is no shortcut to better scoring.
Better golf is attained through
infinite attention to detail.

Doug Ford

What does it take to be a champion?
Desire, dedication, determination,
concentration and the will to win.

Patty Berg

The constant undying hope for
improvement makes golf so
exquisitely worth playing.

Bernard Darwin

WHERE ELSE BUT GOLF?

A tolerable day, a tolerable green, a tolerable opponent, supply (or ought to supply) all that any reasonably constituted human being should require in the way of entertainment. With a fine sea view, and a clear course in front of him, the golfer should find no difficulty in dismissing all worries from his mind. Care may sit behind the horseman, she never presumes to walk with the caddie. No inconvenient reminiscences of the ordinary workaday world, no intervals of weariness or monotony interrupt the pleasures of the game. And of what other recreation can this be said?

A. J. Balfour
Avid golfer and Prime Minister of Britain

Dr. Laidlaw Purves *putting at the Royal Wimbledon Club, London*

On the Scottish coastal courses
before flagsticks were used,
a sea gull's feather was stuck in
the ground to mark the hole.

Reading a green is like
reading the small type in a contract.
If you don't read it with painstaking care,
you are likely to be in trouble.

Claude Hamilton

Putting is like wisdom, partly a natural gift
and partly the accumulation of experience.

Arnold Palmer

Golf was scarcely heard of outside Scotland
until the last half of the 19th century.

Charles Blair MacDonald, *course architect and U.S. Amateur Open Champion 1895*

GOLF IN NORTH AMERICA

While golf balls and clubs were imported from Scotland to Virginia, South Carolina, and Maryland as early as 1734, the first golf clubs formed were farther north. The Montreal Golf Club was formed in 1873, and the first U.S. club was the St. Andrew's Golf Club of Yonkers, New York (1888).

The most notable man behind golf's early explosive growth in America was Charles Blair MacDonald. Having studied at the University of St. Andrews in Scotland, MacDonald also acquired a taste for golf. Upon graduation in 1874, he returned to Chicago, where no golf courses existed. In 1892, he laid out a few holes for friends, and by 1895 he had created a new 18-hole course in Wheaton for the Chicago Golf Club (one of the five founding clubs of the USGA). His most notable course was the National Golf Links in Southampton, opened in 1911.

WHO WILL BE SECOND?

Walter Hagen was golf's earliest colorful character with a flair for the expensive and the dramatic. His bravado was matched only by his short game on the course and his mind games on the opponent. Standing on the first tee of a major tournament, he would loudly say, "I wonder who's going to take second?" People loved him no matter if he won or lost, but most of the time he won. He won two U.S. Opens, four British Opens, five PGA Championships (1921, 1924–27), the Canadian and French Opens once. He beat the best golfers of his day, including Gene Saragen and the young Bobby Jones.

THE AMATEURS

Throughout 1885 to 1914, golf was run by amateurs for amateurs. Professionals were generally from lower social classes and were excluded from any controlling influence on the game. While the amateur golfer was the professional's social superior, he was seldom his golfing superior.

The best British amateurs were John Ball (first amateur to win the Open and winner of the Amateur Championship eight times), Harold Hilton (winner of four Amateurs, two Opens, and one U.S. Amateur), and F. G. Tait (best-loved golfer of his day). The best U.S. amateurs were Francis Quimet and Bobby Jones. After Bobby Jones, the professionals began to dominate golf for good.

POSITIVE THINKING

Golf is more in your mind than in your clubs.

Bruce Crampton

Our best friends and our worst enemies
are our thoughts. A thought can do us more good
than a doctor or a banker or a faithful friend.
It can also do us more harm than a brick.

Dr. Frank Crane

Finally, brothers, whatever is true, noble, right
and admirable—think about these things.

Philippians 4:8

I am an optimist. It does not seem
too much use being anything else.

Winston Churchill

A BAG OF FEATHERS, PLEASE

E arliest golf was played with a "feathery" ball, a round leather case stuffed with feathers. In 1848, the solid gutta-percha ball made from a hard resin was introduced. The new gutta was extremely cheaper and thus made golf available to more than just the rich. However, this was the last time a golf ball would be judged by its price. All future improvements would be designed to increase the distance even if the ball cost more. Haskell Coburn created the wound rubber core ball in 1900. The Haskell dominated the market within a few years because, as *Golf Illustrated* commented in 1902, "No power on earth will deter men from using a ball that will add to the length of their drive."

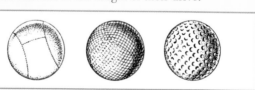

GOLF BETWEEN THE EARS

An astonishing amount of golf—that is, good golf—is played between the ears. We have to think, to concentrate on the stroke, in order to hit the ball correctly. If this were not so I doubt if we should trouble ourselves to play the game.

In the same way, we want our golf courses to make us think. However much we may enjoy whaling the life out of the little white ball, we soon grow tired of playing a golf course that does not give us problems in strategy as well as skill.

Bobby Jones

Bobby Jones' brief career culminated in 1930, when he won the British Amateur, the British Open, the U.S. Amateur, and the U.S. Open.

A GAME OF HONOR

Golf is a game of honor. If you're playing it any other way, you're not getting the fullest satisfaction from it.

Harvey Penick

It is a test of temper, a trial of honour, a revealer of character. It means going into God's out of doors, getting close to nature, fresh air and exercise, a sweeping of mental cobwebs and a genuine relaxation of tired tissues.

David Forgan

Do not gloat when your enemy falls; when he stumbles, do not let your heart rejoice.

Proverbs 24:17

You might as well praise a man for not robbing a bank as to praise him for playing by the rules.

Bobby Jones

GIVING SOMETHING BACK

I owe everything to golf. This is a fact I cannot
or would not deny, and I only hope that as far as
it has been in my power, I have been able to
put something back into the game to help others.

Henry Cotten
British Open Champion 1934, 1937, 1948

Though your riches increase,
do not set your heart on them.

Psalm 62:10

It is not what we take up, but what
we give up that makes us rich.

Henry Ward Beecher

I'm glad to give something back
to the game I love so much.

Byron Nelson

THE GAME OF GOLF

A game of golf is usually played between two, sometimes four friends. Each player tries to urge his golf ball into a special hole in the grass by tapping it with one of his bundle of sticks. When the ball eventually drops into the hole the golfer remembers the number of whacks it took him and, if his friend is watching, writes that number down on his scorecard. After doing this 18 times the friends add up their scores to find the winner. As in receiving a prison sentence, or the news of a multiple birth of offspring, a low number is hoped for. After working out who is the winner, the losers all say "Well done!" and silently accompany their ex-friend back to the clubhouse.

Frank Muir

PERSEVERANCE

Golf is a lot like life.
When you make a decision, stick with it.

Byron Nelson

Persistent people begin their success
where others end in failure.

Edward Eggleston

Blessed is the man who perseveres under trial,
because when he has stood the test, he will
receive the crown of life that God has promised.

James 1:12

Great works are performed not by strength
but by perseverance.

Samuel Johnson

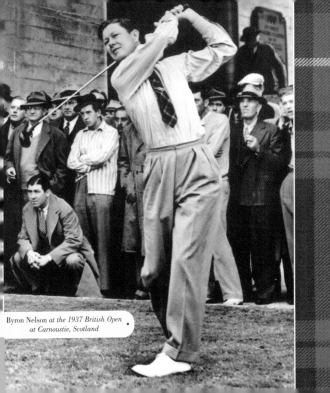

Byron Nelson *at the 1937 British Open at Carnoustie, Scotland*

A GREAT BUNDLE OF STICKS

Until 1938, a tournament golfer could use as many clubs as he could pay for or his caddy could carry. But in that year, the USGA imposed a 14-club limit, and the R & A approved the same number the next year. These changes were made so that the best player could win, not the person with the largest supply of clubs for every possible situation.

GOLF— A GAME FOR ALL

It is a sport in which
the whole American
family can participate—
fathers and mothers,
sons and daughters alike.
It offers healthy respite
from daily toil,
refreshment of body
and mind.

Dwight Eisenhower

Babe Didrikson Zaharias *(1944),*
• *one of the greatest women golfers* •
and athletes of all time

SHATTERED ILLUSIONS

If ever I had illusions about this wonderful game of golf, they have gone. At one time I thought I knew all about golf and how to play it; I had my own ideas as to how I could become proficient, and I believed that I had achieved a certain measure of success. Then I played in my first competition, and all my ideals were shattered, and I wandered in a maze of bewilderment almost like a man blindfolded in a wood, stumbling here and falling there, brought down by my own assurance. Sometimes I was discouraged as I realised the magnitude of the task before me, and only when at last I followed a trail which had been blazed by those who had gone before, could I see the foot of the sunny hill which might lead to success.

Henry Cotten, *Three-time British Open Champion*

THE POWER OF EXAMPLE

There are two things the players on tours
should realize: Adults will copy your swing,
and young people will follow your example.

Harvey Penick

Keep yourself clean and bright; you are
the window through which the world sees God.

Anonymous

A person who lives right, and is right,
has more power in his silence
than another has by words.

Phillips Brooks

In everything set an example
by doing what is good.

Titus 2:7

WOMEN'S GOLF

While golf has never been as actively pursued by women as by men, women have shown both an interest and proficiency in the game for many years. Mary, Queen of Scots, was supposedly a keen golfer. The Royal Musselburgh Golf Club first held a tournament for women in 1867, and the St. Andrews Ladies' Golf Club was founded that same year. The early growth of women's golf was hindered by the powerful effect of inconducive female fashions and male disdain. However, by 1899 there were 128 ladies' golf clubs in Britain.

Hogan, *1951 U.S. Open Champion* •

HOW TO WIN THE OPEN

When Ben Hogan won the U.S. Open in 1951 (the third of his four Opens), he was asked by a reporter for his secret for winning. Hogan caustically replied, "Shoot a lower score than everybody else."

Hogan believed that golf reporters consistently asked stupid questions and could not observe anything for themselves. On one occasion he remarked, "If someone dropped an atom bomb on the sixth hole, the press would wait for a golfer to come in and tell them about it."

PUTT OR PRAY

Prayer never seems to work
for me on the golf course.
I think this has something to do
with my being a terrible putter.

Billy Graham

I never pray to God to make a putt. I pray to
God to help me react good if I miss a putt.

Chi Chi Rodriguez

I never pray that I may win. I just ask
for the courage to do my best.

Gary Player

There are two things you can do with
your head down—play golf and pray.

Lee Trevino

FOOTPRINTS IN THE SAND TRAPS OF LIFE

A man leaves all kinds of footprints when he walks through life. Some you can see, like his children and his house. Others are invisible, like the prints he leaves across other people's lives: the help he gives them and what he has said—his jokes, gossip that has hurt others, encouragement. A man doesn't think about it, but everywhere he passes, he leaves some kind of mark.

M. L. Runbeck ·

A NIBLICK TO THE HEAD

If your opponent is playing several shots in vain attempts to extricate himself from a bunker, do not stand near him and audibly count his strokes. It would be justifiable homicide if he wound up his pitiable exhibition by applying his niblick [the older name for a 9 iron] to your head.

Harry Vardon

SAM SNEAD ON GOLF

The fairways were so narrow you had to
walk down them single file.

You know those two-foot downhill putts
with a break? I'd rather see a rattlesnake.

If I'da cleared the trees and drove the green,
it woulda been a great tee shot.

These greens are so fast I have to hold my putter
over the ball and hit it with the shadow.

There's an old saying: If a man comes home with
sand in his cuffs and cockleburs in his pants,
don't ask him what he shot.

• Sam Snead *lines up a putt at 1939 Masters* •

ST. ANDREWS—
STILL THE STANDARD

While the beginnings of golf are shrouded in the green glens and misty lochs of Scotland long before 1457, we do know that the game has been played at the Royal and Ancient Golf Club of St. Andrews for over 500 years. As golf's earliest shrine, St. Andrews is still the standard. For an amateur, merely playing the Old Course is a lifetime quest. For professionals, winning the Open at St. Andrews is the ultimate achievement.

ILLUSTRATION CREDITS

Brownlow Private Collection:
7, 11, 12, 17, 20, 22, 26, 57, 62, 63.

Hobbs Golf Collection: 15, 37.

Ralph W. Miller Golf Library:
33, 39, 45, 49, 54, 61.

Wood River Gallery:
Cover, 8, 21, 25, 28, 30, 40, 46, 53, 58.